# DIE LEERE MITTE

*Random Access Journal*

## BERLIN

Issue n.3 ¬ 08/2019
30°C ¬ 52.4802743 ¬ 13.5441468

```
#include <stdio.h>
int main()
{
printf("Hello, Berlin!");
return 0;
}
```

DIE LEERE MITTE
*Guidelines*

**Broadly accepted:** Experimental and conceptual writing, theo-retical papers, asemic and concrete texts, vispo, theorems, axiom collection, quantum weirdness, reviews of books addressing these topics and the like.

**Texts:** poetry (60 lines max. overall); prose (500-600 words max. overall). *Format*: Times New Roman 12; single line spacing; all in one .doc or .odt file. *Languages*: Catalan, Croatian, English, French, German, Italian, Russian, Spanish.

**Visual:** 1-3 B&W images. *Format*: jpg, tiff, png, 72-300 DPI.

Simultaneous submissions are welcome, provided that the piece is withdrawn if accepted elsewhere, as well as previously published works when properly credited. Each issue will be free to download (.pdf). A printed version will be made available through lulu.com for collectors. No reading fee; no payment or copies to contributors at present. Authors assume responsibility for the originality, intel-lectual property rights and ethical implications of submitted works.

submissions: leeremittemag@gmail.com
home: https://leserpent.wordpress.com/category/dlm/
twitter: @ LeereMitte

Edited in Berlin by Horst Berger and Federico Federici.
ISBN 9798646313363

# Contents

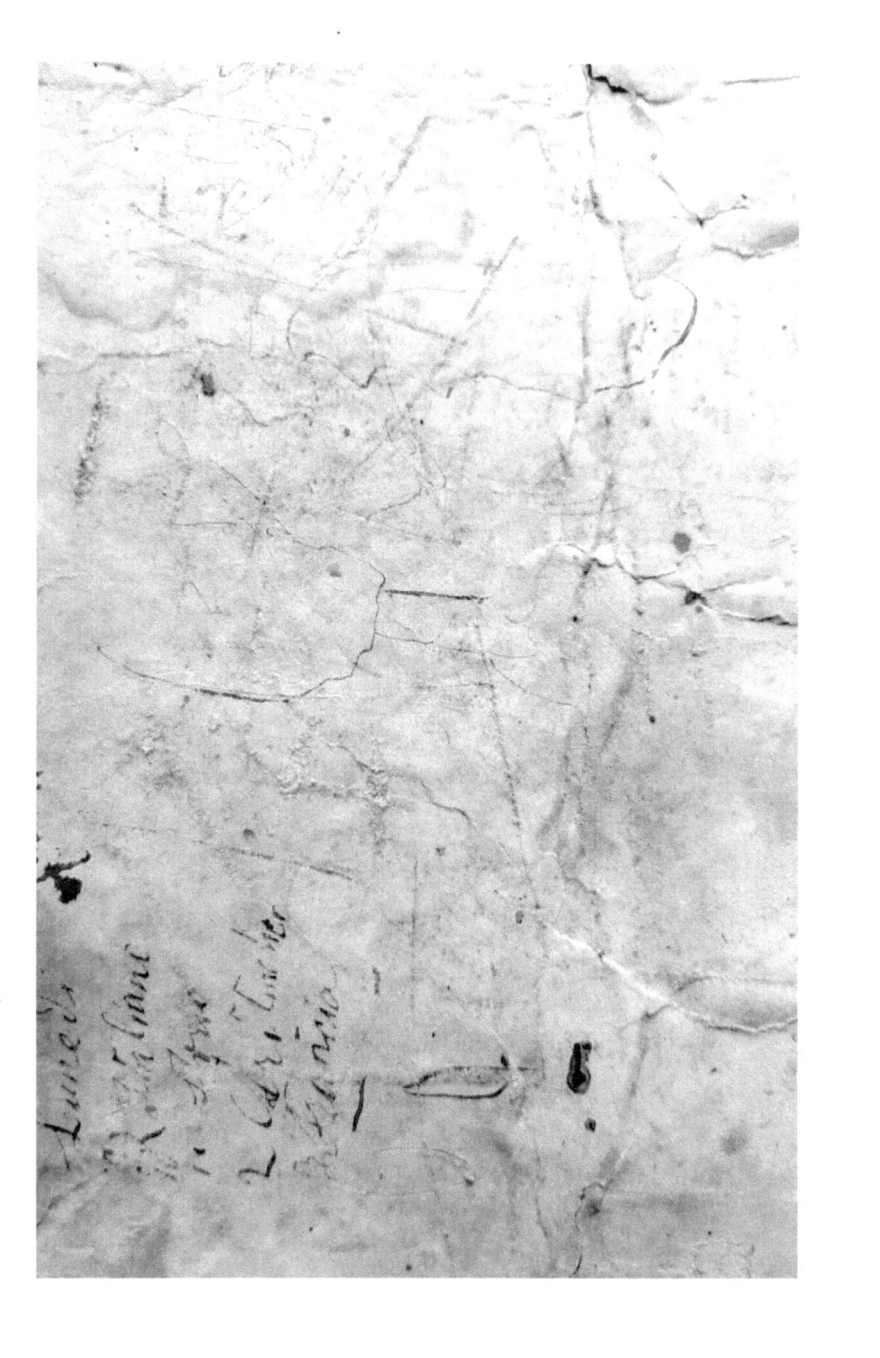

So many double agents have gone

I just respond better to people

The soundtrack of tonal inflection and guitars

Talking, talking around me

Man is meant to have arguments

If you think too long, you think wrong

Something about audio metaphors

That structure there goes like this and this and this −
I thought I invented that

They steal big computers. The devil is in the moon and has
large wings.
The devils go anywhere

My fingers don't say anything.
My fingers don't talk

Not very Jerry
Not very obbligato

There's a science to openness

One of these lucky days I'll be dead
One of these lucky days will change everything

He attracted some attention when he found the fourth
dimension

Agendas in forms of seeing.
To weaponize seeing and cajoling with radical statistics

Putting yourself in a position to see things.
Different things. To see differences, slight variations of the
original

It starts with one person taking a leap and another person
catching  that person.
Over and over, taking turns till the impulse to leap softens and
quiet engulfs all

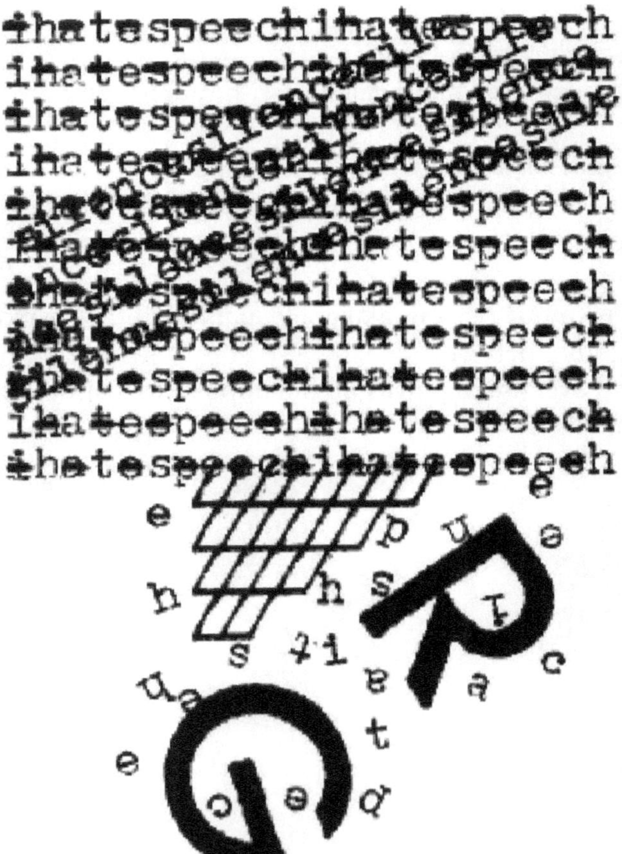
ihatespeechihatespeech

```
                springandall
               nspringandall
              onspringandall
             ponspringandall
            uponspringandall
           suponspringandall
          d suponspringandall
         nd suponspringandall
        end suponspringandall
       pend suponspring andall
      epend suponspringandall
     depend suponspringandall
    hdepend suponspringandall
   chdepend suponspringandall
  uchdepend suponspringandall
 muchdepend suponspringandall
omuchdepend suponspringandall
somuchdepend suponspringandall
```

firstfontbestfont
firstfontbestfont
firstfontbestfont
firstfontbestfont
firstfontbestfont
firstfontbestfont
firstfontbestfont
firstfontbestfont
firstfontbestfont

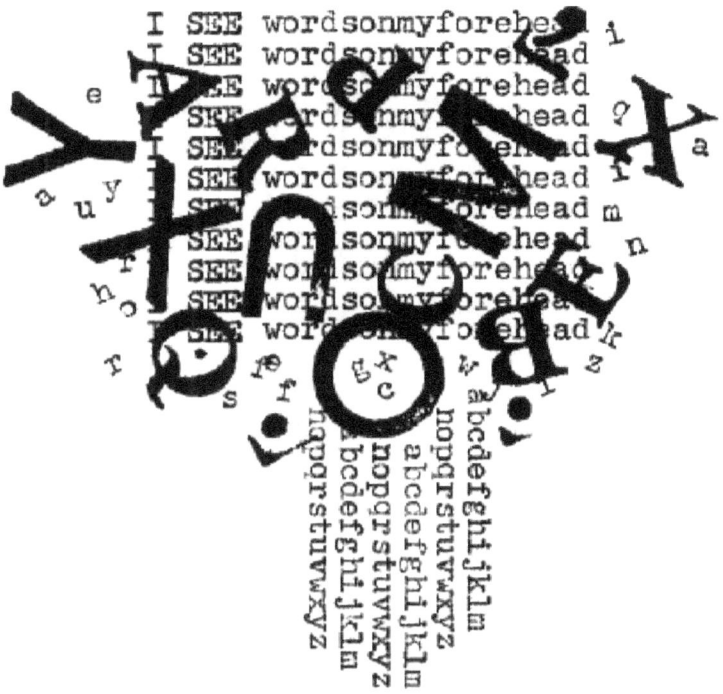

```
butinthings
butinthings
butinthings
butinthings
butinthings
butinthings
butinthings
butinthings
noideasbutinthings
```

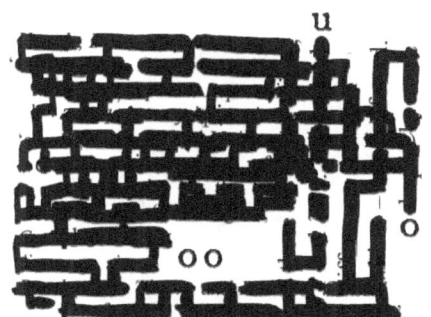

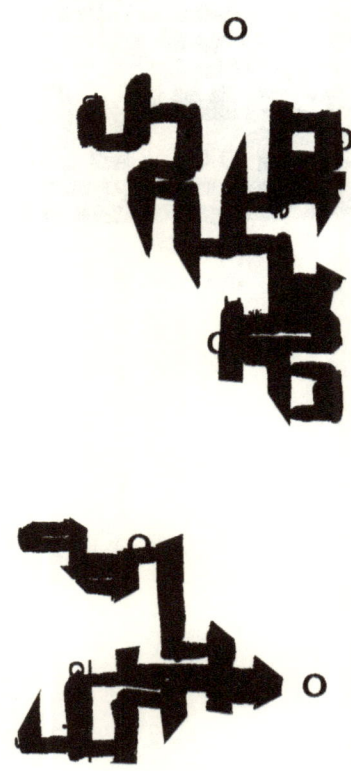

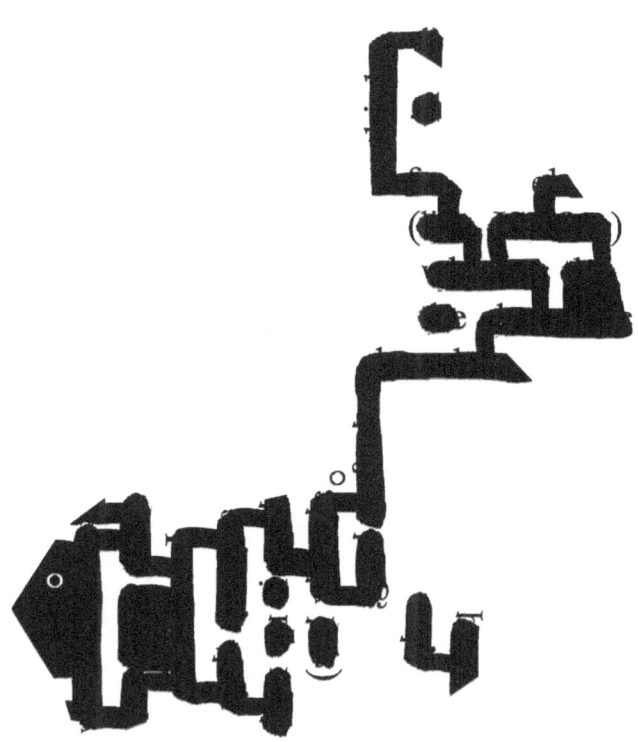

Ethiopia is a month
in january
mexico is a month
in january
october is a month
in hong kong
japan is in the spring
rome is in a
month in fall
i am in the garden
by the herons
i am in the garden
by the peacocks
i am in the garden
by the egrets
i am in the garden
by the ravens
i am in the garden
by the pheasants

cave of birthdays,
every wondersome
being happy
tomorrow, Thursday.
we airmake to
religion, trying
to discover
what hand
can hand a
story by the cocks
names for white
birds in Arabic
after the pantomime
looking anyway
at the shuffle
diagonal way
to fall into
crevices of
making tiny
ways to fall into
making tiny pots
ways to fall into
making tiny leaves
ways to fall into
faking tiny plants
ways to fall into
making tiny cacti
ways to fall into
ways to fall into
ways to fall into
making the into world
making the into world

making the into world
musical of music
lime samfestingar
statue of liberty
a hue of green
ways to fall into

```
          .
          .
          .
          .
          i
          i
          i
          i
          I
          I
          I
          I
          I am
          I am
          I am
          I am
          I am am I
          I am am I
          I am am I
          I am am I
               am I
               am I
               am I
               am I
                  I
                  I
                  I
                  I
                  i
                  i
                  i
                  i
                  .
                  .
                  .
                  .
```

# P
# ULPIT
# TULIP
# LITUP

```
        to    get    her
          to   get   her
           to   get   her
            to  get  her
             to get  her
             to get her
              together
              together
              together
              together
             to get her
            to  get  her
           to   get   her
          to    get    her
         to     get    her
        to      get    her
       to       get    her
      to        get     her
     to         get     her
    to          get      her
   to           get      her
  to            get       her
 to             get       her
to              get        her
to              get        her
to              get         her
to              get         her
to              get          her
to              get          her
to              get           her
to              get           her
to              get            her
to              get            her
to              get             her
to              get             her
to              get              her
```

1

6

11

«Nella _ mia_ Officina lavoro a_ una_ *Calligrafia senza scrittura*___
È una Calligrafia a più Dimensioni_ un Vuoto__ Una Memoria_
trasparente_ umile e_ audace_____ Con un Segno vibrante_ rit-
mico_ che_ diventa Tratto_ radica le_ Parole in un_ Pensiero-
non Pensiero___ Partendo dal Cammino_ dai Passi__ Entrando_
nelle Lettere_____ Scarnifico la T_ la M_ la S__ Le apro_ le
vedo_ le esploro_ le penso per abitarle_____ In questi Spazi_
i Colori sono_ Esperienze_ i Punti sono_ estesi___ La Ten-
sione è_ continua nei_ Movimenti del Passaggio_ del Respiro_
dell'Affondo_ del Riposo_ della Lotta_____ Abbraccio_ sento un
Pensiero___ in modo che i Nodi _ scritti_ possano_ indicare _ i
Sensi delle__ Parole_ Il loro_ Radicamento_ nella_ Reciprocità
dei__ nostri Rapporti_ nelle Molecole_ del nostro___ Stare_____
Attraverso Chine_ Fotografie_ Microvideo_ Installazioni e Performance che_ interrogano l'Ambiente_ e_ le Persone coinvolte_
ho sviluppato alcune_ Ricerche_ e_ loro hanno_ trovato_ Me_
tra cui *Stato ai Luoghi*__ Una Performance di Incontri a_ Palermo
e_ in Repubblica Ceca___ *Monitulipare*___ Immagini del verbo
Monitulipare__ Fare della_ Realtà_ frammentata_ un'Apertura
in _ Vuoti che_liberano_ Linee_rette_parallele_____ E_ ultima_
Sia *Rbaria Achidi* _ per _ salvare alcuni_ Punti_ vestendoli di__
Suono_____ Mi_ aspetto Tutto__ Ringrazio_ le Linee_____»

Tommasina Bianca Squadrito

[First appeared in «Istànti» n.12, March 2014.]

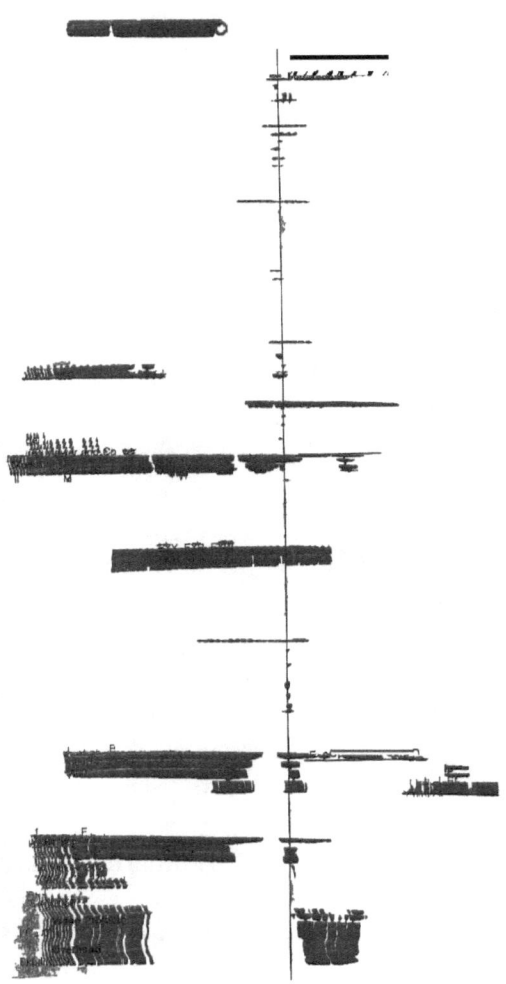

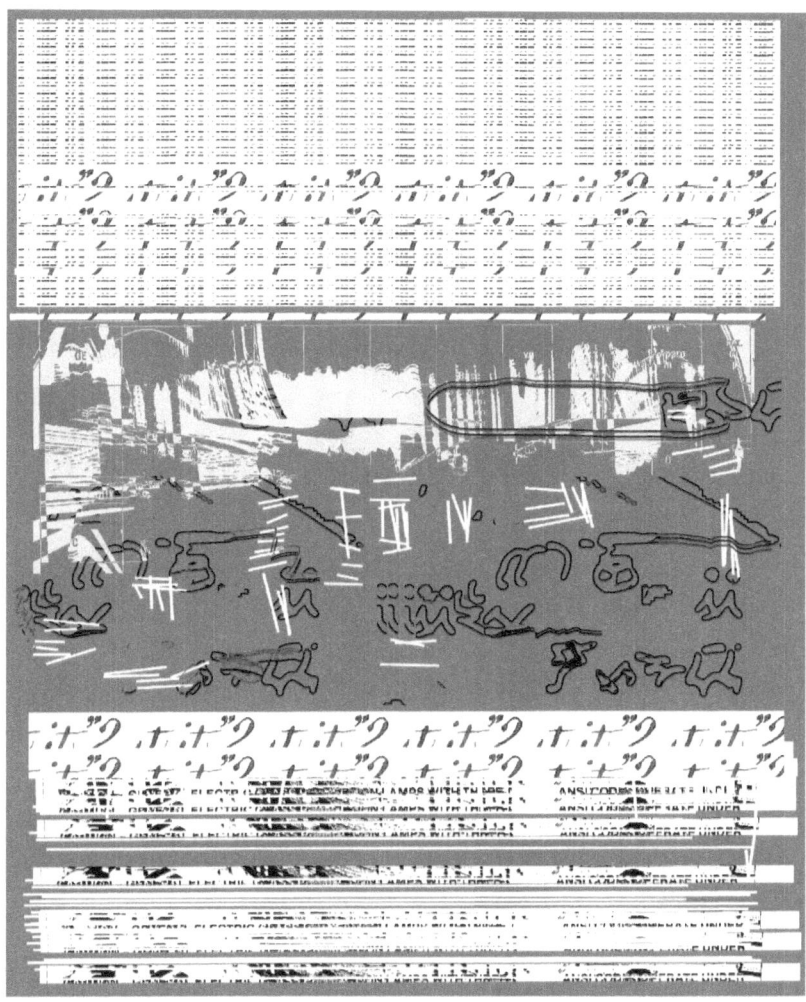

27

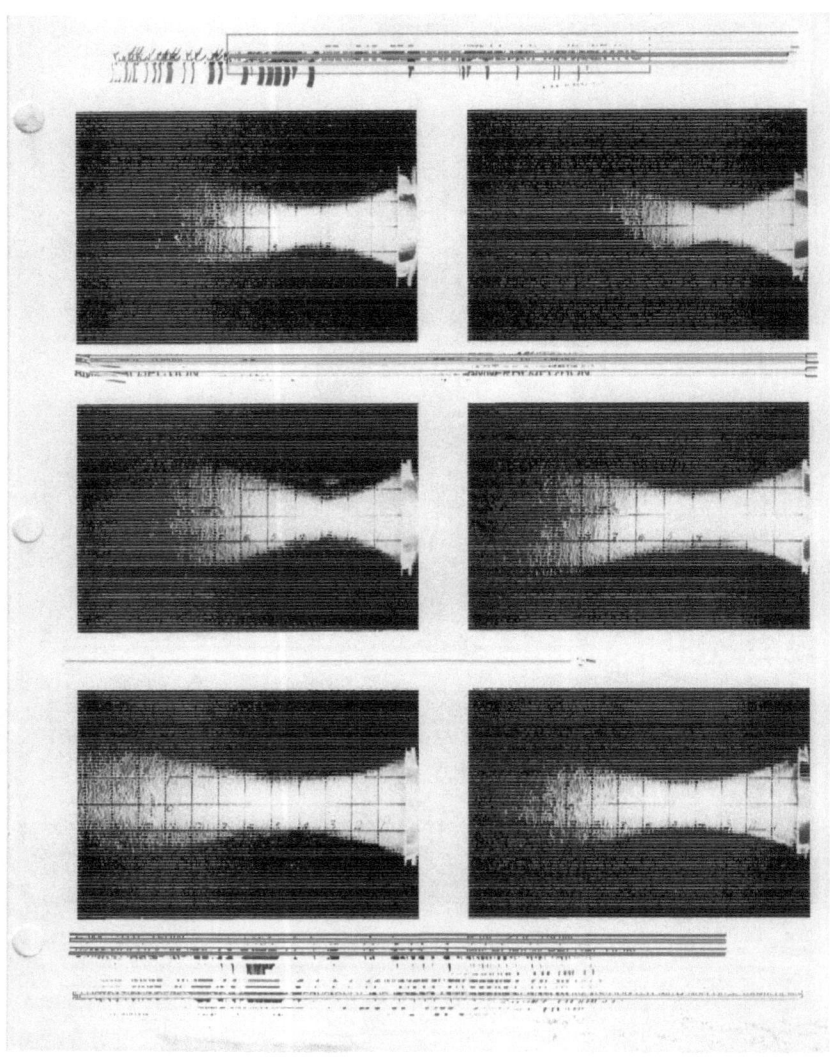

# Alegria Imperial : *un-weighed*

*a river of feet rumbles into my stare*

against furious    bands
of whiteness                              *the flow*

no winking pebbles   or snouts that sigh
ageing suns              *unmoved*

threaded light   poised   to swarm
my breast                              *heaves and dips*

on wind-stirred copper    leaves
a papery moonset    *the soundless roar*

i ram fear-gripped through
barricades                              *to eternity*

your bath's steaming     a wind-whisper
the turn to              *a drizzle-in-cups*

hands that scrape my skin       detritus of
altered states

                              *her words*

the depths of my being wash     into a mud pool
sheathed-thorns in dregs

                    *un-weighed*

Alegria Imperial : *a spy's report*


of what's   found

sifting caked soil   on cracked soles
censured   senses                                      *rambling words*

many-a-nights'   worth
a window's bared   innards                   *tin-laughter*

threadbare birch   stray moons
unhinged                                               *poked chords*

julienned clouds racing   pumped-up eyes
on galaxies                                         *a restless whirring*

stilled in pools for       divination
mud crabs crawl                              *into naked ears*

I, a witness, to the     fall of cotton-souls
in place of death count                *crosses of missing limbs*

nameless sums


[First published at «otata» n.42, June 2019.]

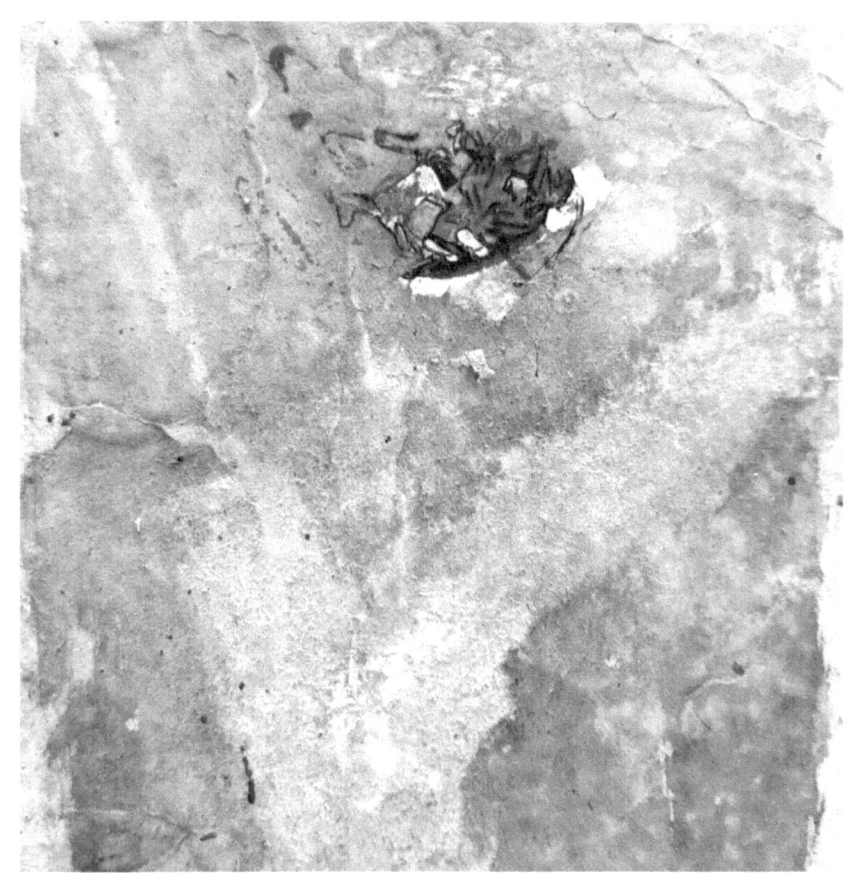